CW01652199

RHYME CRAFT

The North West

Edited By Allie Jones

First published in Great Britain in 2018 by:

Young**Writers**

Young Writers
Remus House
Coltsfoot Drive
Peterborough
PE2 9BF
Telephone: 01733 890066
Website: www.youngwriters.co.uk

Book Design by Ashley Janson

SB ISBN 978-1-78896-146-2
Printed and bound in the UK by BookPrintingUK
Website: www.bookprintinguk.com
YB0346M

FOREWORD

Welcome Reader, to Rhymecraft - The North West.

Among these pages you will find a whole host of poetic gems, built from the ground up by some wonderful young minds. Included are a variety of poetic styles, from amazing acrostics to creative cinquains, from dazzling diamantes to fascinating free verse.

Here at Young Writers our objective has always been to help children discover the joys of poetry and creative writing. Few things are more encouraging for the aspiring writer than seeing their own work in print. We are proud that our anthologies are able to give young authors this unique sense of confidence and pride in their abilities as well as letting their poetry reach new audiences.

The editing process was a tough but rewarding one that allowed us to gain an insight into the blooming creativity of today's primary school pupils. I hope you find as much enjoyment and inspiration in the following poetry as I have, so much so that you pick up a pen and get writing!

Allie Jones

CONTENTS

THE POEMS

Four Seasons

(Haiku poetry)

Budding trees, green leaves
Beautiful butterflies fly
It is springtime now.

The sun's bright yellow,
Colourful flowers bloom up
Summer has begun.

Dull, grey, cloudy skies,
Orange trees and crunchy leaves,
Now autumn has come.

Glittering, soft snow
Snowflakes falling on bare trees,
Now winter is here.

Abdur-Rahmaan Razzaq (5)

The Blossoms Of Our World

Earth is a cherry blossom tree
For both grow strong
And both fall down
But you only have one life
So cherish it.

Our world is a mountain
And full of beauty
There are great things to overcome
Complicated challenges
Times will be hard but persevere.

The world is a rainforest
Full of adventure
You can go skiing in the Alps
Or go snorkelling on the Great Barrier Reef
But make the most of it.

Earth is a leopard
It springs out of nowhere
And you never know what's around the corner

There are surprises, good and bad.
But
Have fun!

Sofia Samar Riaz (9)

Untitled

To build or not to build?
That is the question.
Wood or stone?
Quartz or clay?
Diamond or emerald?
Building is the way to start.

To mine or not to mine?
With a diamond pick or an iron one;
Break the ore,
Gain XP
Mining is the way to be.

To craft or not to craft?
Make decorations and stuff.
Create weapons and armour
To defeat a skeleton or Creeper
Fight the Ender Dragon
And end with the Wither.

This is Minecraft
The never-ending game

Full of possibilities
With a lot of fame.

Fatema Nazri (10)

Cheetham CE Community Academy, Cheetham Hill

The Wise Man!

Once a wise man said,
'Always brush your teeth before bed
Otherwise you'll end up with yellow teeth,
And your breath will smell like rotten beef.
Make sure you look after them,' he began to say.
I could see from his mouth,
That his had fallen out.
As the wise man continued to talk,
I made my escape,
As I started two walk
I could see he was just trying to be nice,
So I thanked the wise man,
For his kind advice.

Saffa Waseem (10)
Cheetham CE Community Academy, Cheetham Hill

Survival Game Mode

When you mine at night
Don't stay too long
There might be Creepers in sight.

I put on diamond armour
In the Nether portal I go
It might be scary, I'll mine Nether ore.

In a cave I am
Carving eye of Enders
It's scary, dark and dim.

I've found an end portal
I'm placing eye of Enders
'I've made it!' I shout.

Sameen Dur-e (8)
Cheetham CE Community Academy, Cheetham Hill

Family Actions

(Haiku poetry)

Siblings do kind things
Letting you enjoy the day
Or annoying you.

Parents are caring
They help you with your homework
Or work in the day.

Cousins come over
Visiting the family
Running and playing.

Aunties make you food
Preparing the meals for us
Serving it to all.

Rayhan Raza (10)
Cheetham CE Community Academy, Cheetham Hill

My Way Of Freedom - What's Yours?

F reedom means
R ights to have your own choice and say
E ven when you think it's
E specially about you, you still
D eserve a chance to be free
n **O** matter what
M y way of freedom is writing poems, what's yours?

Sufyaan Shafqat (10)
Cheetham CE Community Academy, Cheetham Hill

Enderman

Their spacey eyes,
If you stare, you'll die.
I'm describing the Enderman
Cooler than spray tan,
This is not a lie.

Haleema Saleem (10)
Cheetham CE Community Academy, Cheetham Hill

War

War
army, military,
soldier, captain, general,
fighting, chopper, bullets, bombs,
chaos, fear, blood, shock, trauma,
convoy, combat, enemy, trench, shelter, prisoner,
spy, tactics, barricade, alert, battle,
landmine, tanks, dynamite, destruction,
retreat, surrender, relief,
injury, death,
Grave.

Edith Davies (10)
Guilden Sutton CE Primary School, Guilden Sutton

Riding My Bike!

I wake up early it's damp and cold,
It's misty outside but I'm feeling bold,
My kit is ready, my bike's just there,
My father says we can ride anywhere.

I get on my bike, we ride down the lanes,
We're going so fast I feel the pain,
Faster and faster, we race through the wind,
The sun's coming out, what a great blend!

There's hills in the distance, they're creeping up fast,
The climb is so steep but I make it at last.
What a challenge, I've made it, I'm finally there,
The view is amazing, I take a minute to stare.

Esme Rose Al-Kadhimi (10)
Guilden Sutton CE Primary School, Guilden Sutton

Snow

Snow
Cold, white flakes, falling on the
Trees' bare branches.
This Arctic winter's day
Ice, icicles, long spikes
Shivering in the
Heatless sun. Freezing
Shivering
Cold
Snow.

James Rogers (10)
Guilden Sutton CE Primary School, Guilden Sutton

War!

(A diamante poem)

Bombarding,
rifles, bullets,
burning, crying, aching,
disaster, shrapnel, shells, toxic,
dissolving, mutilating, swelling,
suffering, spasm,
Lifeless.

Ioana Ursoi (10)
Guilden Sutton CE Primary School, Guilden Sutton

Thunder And Lightning

(A diamante poem)

Lightning
bright, sudden
flashing, shining, shocking,
explosive, powerful, loud, deafening,
booming, crashing, rumbling,
banging, terrifying
thunder.

Finlay Noble (10)
Guilden Sutton CE Primary School, Guilden Sutton

Homework And Fun

(A diamante poem)

Homework,
hard, long,
frustrating, boring, puzzling,
books, shapes, games, videos,
entertaining, exciting, interesting,
enjoyable, active,
fun!

Marcus Badiru (10)
Guilden Sutton CE Primary School, Guilden Sutton

War

(A diamante poem)

War
deadly, dangerous,
shouting, screaming, shaking
blood, bodies, saviours, survivors
healing, hallucinating, heroic
rest, recuperate
peace.

Oliver Owens (10)
Guilden Sutton CE Primary School, Guilden Sutton

War And Destruction

War
loud, bang,
bang, gun, fire,
trenches, water, destructions around,
devastation, starvation, homeless,
houses flattened,
destruction.

Declan Jones (10)
Guilden Sutton CE Primary School, Guilden Sutton

Scars

Cannons,
devastating, scary,
explosive, danger, anger,
guns, tanks, knives, men,
firing, blasting, cold,
despair, sacrifice,
terror.

Callum Little (10)

Guilden Sutton CE Primary School, Guilden Sutton

War

(A diamante poem)

War,
boom, crash,
dying, marching, hurting,
Hitler, soldiers, Churchill, women,
terrorising, fighting, crying,
frozen, dead,
sirens.

Isabelle Grace Jones (10)
Guilden Sutton CE Primary School, Guilden Sutton

War

(A diamante poem)

War,
loud, horrific,
exploding, deafening, fuming,
flames, bombs, trenches, guns,
screaming, blazing, living,
loud, horrific,
war.

Maggie Puleston-Davies (10)
Guilden Sutton CE Primary School, Guilden Sutton

Swans

Swans,
sparkly white,
quacking, running, swimming,
feathers, beaks, wings,
flying, fighting,
dangerous, deadly
swans.

Matthew Randles (11)
Guilden Sutton CE Primary School, Guilden Sutton

Bang!

War,
danger, fighting,
bang, bang, gone,
aim, battle, defence, destroy,
kind, friendly, nice,
together, team,
peace.

Hannah Boyles (10)
Guilden Sutton CE Primary School, Guilden Sutton

Nits, Nits!

Nits, nits what horrible things!
They hatch into lice and nibble your skin.
They dance and prance and swing through your hair,
But cause an itch that's hard to bear,
I itch all day and I itch all night
I can't stand their awful bite.
Then comes the killer spray and drowns them in fright!

Vamousse, Lyclear and Hedrin,
I've tried them all
But nothing can stop them from having a ball.
I dread the nit comb scratching my head,
But Mum always bring it out just before bed.

Why, oh why is my scalp so tasty?
Dad gets the scissors out, 'Please don't be hasty!'

Nits, nits, what horrible things.

Maisie Nolan (9)
Lady Barn House School, Langlands

The Frog

A small but hairy frog,
Was sat outside a bog
Picking his nose,
And biting his toes.
He was fat, round
And made an atrocious sound,
Ribbit-ribbit-ribbit.
He had big blue eyes
And adored flies.
He ate the flies with his big red tongue
Once he got one he sang a song,
'I'm the nasty old frog
Who lives near to the bog.
I'm surrounded by flies
That sometimes go in my eyes.'
Singing, dancing you name it
'Cause he's not the type who likes to sit.
This is what he likes to do,
He is quite mean though, 'cause he's comin' for you!

Macey Haworth (9)
Lady Barn House School, Langlands

Unicorn Cold

This summer I got a cold but no ordinary one at all,
It started when I was playing with a unicorn horn.
It began with a cough but with marshmallow melt,
Then strawberry string wriggled in my tummy as well.
I vomited a rainbow,
Sneezed sparkles,
Pink and blue,
They all ended up in a bowl and made an amazing brew!
I think it started with the unicorn horn,
So I advise you not to use one, even if you dare,
So you don't catch the unicorn cold and take great care.

Ava Wainwright (9)
Lady Barn House School, Langlands

The Unknown

In the deep, dark, dreary Underworld he lies,
Not a soul knows about him,
He has fierce fiery red eyes,
And a blood-red body.
He smells of meat.
Legend says he was previously a happy, cheerful young boy
Who went missing one day...
If you venture near the deep, dark, dreary Underworld,
You will never be seen again!

Aysha Khan (9)
Lady Barn House School, Langlands

Stormy Sea

Sea
deep marine
flowing, whirling, shining
water, sharks, earth, wind
undulating, rolling, curving
bumpy, wooded
land.

Ruma Gupta (9)
Lady Barn House School, Langlands

Fire

It burned me
It hurt me
Pain flooded me
I didn't want to live
I was told to believe
But nothing would
Even though I should
Words cannot describe it
It made my heart pump
It crashes down buildings
It kills lives
And nothing stops it
But its enemy.

Amy Hueting (9)
Lady Barn House School, Langlands

Mythical Creatures

Fire-breathing,
Always seeing,
Flying through the night.
What could this be?
A flying tree?
Can you guess it out right?

A dragon!

Snow is falling in the woods,
All you can hear is the sound of thuds.
Something is stirring,
Get out before they come out.

Humans think they are pretty with coloured lights,
Is Tinkerbelle really like this?
I am not so sure.
So what are they on the forest floor?

Bad fairies!

Sharp, long with a glowing light,
This is enough to give you a fright.

Approaches a maiden without any fear,
Maybe she wishes she wasn't here.

On four hooves, it leaves no trail,
Pure white like a ship's sail.
The horn is surrounded by magic,
If you get hit, it might end up tragic.

So what is this mysterious creature?
Can you guess it from my clues?

A friendly unicorn!

Morwenna Hughes (9)
Liscard Primary School, Wallasey

Rhymecraft

I don't like doing Rhymecraft
But I do like playing Minecraft.

Enderman ate my friend's doggy,
Which made me feel really sorry.
I felt bad for a little while,
So I carried on playing which made me smile.
Steve is so clever,
He can get food from the Nether.
There is not good weather in the Nether.
I dug so deep I found lava,
Which created a drama.

Witches
Potions
Animals
Mobs
Ender Dragon
Withers

It's just a game of blocks
Which I play in my socks.

I like to build houses with traps in
Then I put pigs in.

I don't like doing Rhymecraft
But I do like playing Minecraft.

Ella Summer Casey (9)

Liscard Primary School, Wallasey

Cheer Life!

I am a cheerleader, it is hard work, tumbling and flipping, standing upright
On many hands, trying my best to stay very, very tight.
Our team name is Nitros Elite
Because I know I work harder than any football guy, if you say I'm not an athlete
Get ready for what's up next
Because what you're about to meet is the best of the best.
I am a flying through the air
Hitting my stunt then flicking my hair
Ensuring our facials are cute at the judge, to make sure we get the highest score
But we say in our heads, 'More, more, more.'
Our three minute routine is over, our hard work paid off, another medal, another trophy we won together, however no time to rest
Because we are determined to stay the best.

Amy Smyth (9)
Liscard Primary School, Wallasey

The Emerald Forest

Extraordinary trees so high
They can touch the sky.
The forest sounds like a lion roaring.
Like a book waiting to be read by millions of people.
So big it's impossible to explore!
Thousands of nooks and crannies
Where creepy-crawlies live!
A pond that is full of beautiful ducks
In all shapes and sizes!
And it's glistening in the sun
Amazing!
The magnificent flowers smell like a sweet shop
The cool breeze feels relaxing after a long day
So please help look after our forest!

Grace Louise Hopkinson (9)
Liscard Primary School, Wallasey

In The Mine

In a lonely day in Minecraft
You might be sitting in a mineshaft
Tired and bored
You take out your sword
You see mobs are nearby
So you look closely with one eye
Overtaken by fear
You listen with your ear.
Nothing can be seen
Only one thing can be heard
'Footsteps' is the word
Then you run through the hallways
Getting lost in alleyways
You turn the corner
And see a miner
His eyes are white and full of light
You blink and he's gone
By then it's become dawn.
And to this day the legend lives on
Some may decline
To believe in Herobrine

The truth we may never know
But we can make the legend grow.

Ellie Tiera Lomax (9)
Liscard Primary School, Wallasey

Dreams And Wishes

When I was little my dreams were small,
Then my dreams grew nice and tall.
I have parties and get lots of toys,
But lots of toys make such a noise.

In just one day everything changed, my dreams were real
We had a new family, which meant a great deal.
We had lots of games and fun,
Which we thought would never come.

I now believe I can be a vet,
Another dream not real just yet.
Suddenly all my dreams came
A lovely portrait in a beautiful frame.

Lily-Mae Price (9)
Liscard Primary School, Wallasey

About Me

I like to do things my own way,
Nobody can tell me what to do,
I have an extraordinary mum and dad
And they think I am wonderful too.

I enjoy playing football,
Friends I have many,
I play for the football team Rakers
My manager's name is Kenny.

When I am playing football,
When I am running down the wing,
The Rakers' supporters are shouting
'Come on Noodles!' they all sing
With my blonde curly hair blowing in the wind.

Josh Roberts-Edwards (10)
Liscard Primary School, Wallasey

Goodbye Grandad

An angel came from up above, she called my grandad's name,
'I will free you from all this pain.
No more worrying about things anymore
Step into the light and come in through the door
Your mum is waiting for you.'
'Come close in my arms son and I will guide you through
To a place where you can finally rest,
To find peace and true happiness.'
Sleep tight Grandad, I miss you so much
We will be together again one day and your hand I will touch.

Lauren Hughes (9)
Liscard Primary School, Wallasey

The Big Adventure With Skeletons!

Going on an adventure,
Where will monsters be?
As cold as ice,
The sound of mice,
Hidden under a tree!
Sweaty and hot can't really stop,
The floor so hot it is lava...
Skeleton! Skeleton!
Where is he now?
Oh no I have just found a broken bough.
Sticks and stones, hidden old bones wherever you go,
Can't stop, won't stop, oh no,
Hurry up, hurry up, we really need to go,
There is a skeleton behind me, run and go!

Chloe Slatter-West (10)
Liscard Primary School, Wallasey

Crystal Clear

In the dark night, nothing's in sight,
The crystals shine bright
They beat the night in wonder
All the people stop and stare and say
'Crystal shine bright tonight
Shine in light just like it's bright.'
As clear as day, they shine so bright
The sun is so light
But it can't beat the crystals
As they shimmer in the night.
It's never too late to be strong
Be clear as a crystal my dear.

Paige Ison (9)
Liscard Primary School, Wallasey

Elf On The Shelf

The Elf on the Shelf is a suspicious guy,
He is called Santa's Special Spy.
Watching out from his shelf of wood,
Making sure we are all being good.
Think twice before you throw a strop,
As your gifts may not leave Santa's workshop.
Don't forget if you want presents on Christmas Day,
Behave yourself whilst you play.
If you don't want the Elf's report to be bad,
Don't be cheeky to Mum or Dad!

Lily Stanley (9)
Liscard Primary School, Wallasey

Seasons To Me Are...

Summer is fun when you can play in the sun
Splashing, hiding and tagging.
Autumn is chilly when you play in the park
Catching conkers, throwing leaves and walking with my family.
Winter is relaxing because you can snuggle under a blanket
Drinking hot chocolate, opening Secret Santas and watching DVDs.
Spring is bright and friendly because you can play out
Kicking a football, walking my dog and making a den.

Will Jones (9)
Liscard Primary School, Wallasey

Playing In The Park

On Friday night I went to the park,
I stayed so late it was really dark.
I was playing with the ball,
One little trip and I had a fall.

I passed the ball to my friend
And then I ran round the bend.
I won the game, what a laugh,
While my old dad took a photograph.

I helped my team
And they seemed so mean
When I got the football strip
I was so excited I did a flip.

Katie Barker (9)
Liscard Primary School, Wallasey

Night Of Disturbance!

He wakes me up at night, keeps a racket in my head,
While I'm trying to sleep in my snuggly bed!

Even though he's my friend and I'll love him to the end
He still drives me round the bend!

He eats really loud, and sounds like a crowd,
He rustles all night until daylight.

And when I'm at school, he sleeps all day,
Then at night it's play, play, play!

Layla Stuart (9)
Liscard Primary School, Wallasey

Climbing Up A Mountain

I am climbing up a mountain, climb, climb, climb,
Quickly, quickly we are running out of time.
The skies are darkening and zombies spawning too
Stars are appearing and the sky's no longer blue.
I hear villagers shouting for help, help, help,
Pigs and cows are snorting and mooing, saying
yelp, yelp, yelp!
I'm at the top now, I'm safe, safe, safe,
I run in a house to meet my mate.

Hugo Jack McCormack-Sell (9)
Liscard Primary School, Wallasey

Fantastic Friends!

B elieve in each other
E xchange silly stories
S hare favourite clothes
T ell it like it is

F ind the answers
R ely on each other
I nspire bravery
E ncourage dreams
N ever stop caring
D evise crazy schemes
S tand by each other.

I love my friends to the moon and back.

Pippa Towns (9)
Liscard Primary School, Wallasey

Food

This is a rhyme, sorry about the time,
This is about food, I'm not trying to be rude.
I love apple crumble, it makes my tummy rumble
I love beans but I hate smelly sardines.
I really like doughnuts and sweets for dessert
I would have lemon drops and swirly lollipops
I like my food roasted but I like toast toasty
What I don't like most, is my mum's chicken roast.

Poppy Coburn (9)
Liscard Primary School, Wallasey

My Acrostic Poem About Britain

B e careful when you go outside, you may want a raincoat
R oast dinners are nice after a long Sunday
I n summer it's too hot, in winter it's too cold
T he Tower of London was founded in 1066
A trip to London would be very nice
I love the Harry Potter books, what about you?
N ice to meet you, would you like a cup of tea?

Hollie McNab (9)
Liscard Primary School, Wallasey

Minecraft Is Cool

When I get grass I use it for my path
Minecraft is my favourite game
But some people think it's really lame.
I play on it when I come home from school
The characters are really cool.
There are so many things to build
All of the budgies get killed.
Playing Minecraft is my favourite thing to do
So you should get the game too.

Jamie Riley (9)
Liscard Primary School, Wallasey

Fantastic Football

Fantastic football is great, when you are at the match it's ecstatic,
Hi, I am a boy and football is what I enjoy.
I support Liverpool and whoever doesn't is a fool.
You can only kick it in the match,
However goalkeepers are allowed to catch.
Liverpool is a professional team,
When you're at the match it's a great scene.

Joe Bennett (9)
Liscard Primary School, Wallasey

Blocks

B uilders building with blocks high in the sky
L ook out for clouds, don't jump... or you will cry
O ut in the distance blocks are high
C old below, how high, let's go back down from the sky
K iss your imagination goodnight, soon stars fill the sky
S ound asleep, soon to build, goodbye.

Lucas Eric Wardman (9)
Liscard Primary School, Wallasey

British Weather!

On Monday it was sunny,
On Tuesday it was dull,
On Wednesday it was cloudy like cloudy lemonade,
On Thursday it was so sunny I nearly turned blind,
On Friday it was raining like the sky was crying,
On Saturday there was icy-cold hailstones,
On Sunday there was more rain
That made us frown because the weekend was over.

Meredith Williams (9)
Liscard Primary School, Wallasey

The Lightning Runner

Powerful and fast, he sneaks through the grass with big bold spots
The hungrier he gets the longer his prey feels
Lions and leopards growl to show they are on the prowl
Don't touch it or you'll get dotted
Don't make it laugh or you'll get spotted.
I am great and bold
I am the best cheetah of them all.

George Clay (9)
Liscard Primary School, Wallasey

Life In Minecraft

Digging through the day into the night,
I found a diamond sword with a bit of a fright.
With this I can slay
Herobrine and his army far, far away.

Building through the day into the night,
I built a big house for somewhere to stay
In the world of Minecraft
Is where I want to stay.

Harvey Farrington (9)
Liscard Primary School, Wallasey

Ender Dragon

As I fly along the way
The Ender Dragon comes out to play.
With his long black tail
And his large, big wings
He pops up! Then takes a dive.
You really have nowhere to hide.
Out of nowhere he often comes
To destroy stuff along the way
Just for you to still stay and play.

Ty Chapman (9)
Liscard Primary School, Wallasey

Starry Night

Diamonds, diamonds shine so bright,
Just like a shooting star,
In the middle of the night.
Stars that twinkle oh so bright,
Diamonds in the middle that blind you like the light.
Lying on your back,
Looking at the stars,
Wondering if there could be life on Mars.

Lily Neve Langley (9)
Liscard Primary School, Wallasey

Friendship Is Cool

I met a little frog and said, 'How do you do?
My name is Hopper, is that your name too?'
'My name is Leaper, that's what I do all day.'
But when I tried to pick him up Leaper ran away.
Roses are red, frogs are cool
Now we have got one here at school!

Grace Ellen Furber (9)
Liscard Primary School, Wallasey

Gold

Like a creeper in the night,
Trying to cause a fright,
That won't work
Because I'll run to the light.

Only one goal,
Mining is life
Life is mining
On the edge of a tunnel
I have a finding
Gold! Can it be?
Yes, finally!

Max Templeton (9)
Liscard Primary School, Wallasey

Furry Friends

There were two little mice
Who were very nice
And they pecked and wrecked
While sitting on a deck.

One called Mickey, he was really mean
While Veronica was as sweet as a queen.
While Veronica squealed with fright,
Mickey jumped with delight.

Imogen Smyth (9)
Liscard Primary School, Wallasey

Minecraft Is So Daft

Minecraft, it's like a mineshaft, creative and daft
Play it fast, play it slow
It's always fun wherever you go.
Build it small, it's always fun to build them all
Countryside green and spiralling city, town grey and tall
Minecraft has got it all.

Emma Smith (9)
Liscard Primary School, Wallasey

My Favourite Pet

I had a big fat cat
It once ate my hat
It was the smartest pet
It once hit the ball into the net.

He creeps around very stealthy
You may believe he's wealthy.
He's my dream team pet
He's the nicest pet I've ever met.

Lily Heaven (9)
Liscard Primary School, Wallasey

Football Dreams

Green grassy field,
Goal on each side,
Player versus player,
Team versus team,
Derbies and El Clásicos
Coaches shouting loudly
Referees blowing whistles soundly
Fans cheering wildly
Waiting for the ball to hit the back of the net.

Jessica Jordan (9)
Liscard Primary School, Wallasey

Faraway Land

Playing in the sand,
As it covers my hand,
In the distance I can see land,
Looking across the ocean,
I fill with emotion.
Who is out there?
Breathing in that sea-salted air,
Not that I know,
Not that I care...

Maddison Georgia Hudson (10)
Liscard Primary School, Wallasey

Gymnastics

G reatness
Y ou can do it
M oving
N ever say never
A cro
S kills
T uck backs
I llusion
C an't is not a word
S ide somersaults.

Grace Evans (10)
Liscard Primary School, Wallasey

Minecraft

M ining is fun
I ndestructible
N ever-ending and
E xciting
C rafting
R unning from mobs
A mazing, it's
F antastic and so
T errific.

Olivia Carney (9)
Liscard Primary School, Wallasey

Night Night

Bright
light, burning
sparkly, shiny, sly
dark night
nothingness.

Thomas Hamilton (9)
Liscard Primary School, Wallasey

Minecraft

M inecraft
I s the best because
N ether end
E nderman
C reeper
R iver raft
A nimals everywhere
F orests
T rees and leaves.

Maisie Leigh Reeves (9)
Liscard Primary School, Wallasey

My Mansion

I live in a mansion as high as the moon,
I have a block of diamonds in every room.
I have an oven, a microwave and a vacuum,
Although I need to clean with a broom,
I also have a pet Mooshroom.

Logan-Lewis Shakespeare (9)
Liscard Primary School, Wallasey

People Vs Minecraft

I was playing with my big cousin Max
And he got out his big pickaxe.

I was so bored
So I polished my gleaming sword.

I made a house and let it be TNT.

Zac Ostensen (9)
Liscard Primary School, Wallasey

Horrible Hobbies

I scored a goal
In the hole
And shouted, 'Whoo!'
The crowd cheered
And launched flares.
The referee blew the whistle
And pricked his finger on a thistle.

Shay Anthony Peter Dilworth (10)
Liscard Primary School, Wallasey

Minecraft

M inecraft
I ndestructible
N ever mine at night
E agerly
C rafting
R ebuild
A pples
F ly
T ime.

Mason Ellis Jackson (10)
Liscard Primary School, Wallasey

Fabulous Minecraft

M ine
I have eyes
N ight
E nder eyes
C raft
R etreat
A pples
F inding diamonds
T reasure.

André Eusebio (9)
Liscard Primary School, Wallasey

Bungle

(A limerick poem)

There was once a sloth called Bungle
Who lived in a deep, dark jungle.
He had nothing to say,
Never wanted to play
Which made all of his friends grumble.

Madison McGuire (10)
Liscard Primary School, Wallasey

Football Life

F riends
O pposition
O n target
T eamwork
B rilliant skills
A ttack
L egend
L eague.

Rhys Jacob Ashby (9)
Liscard Primary School, Wallasey

The True Creeper

Be careful as you build your homes
For the creeper
As in the dark and gloomy night he roams
The bricks of your world.

Lewis Townley (9)
Liscard Primary School, Wallasey

A Recipe For Boo Bear's Family...

Add one hard-working dada
And one beautiful reliable mama
Whisk in a thoughtful daddy

Preheat with unconditional love

Add a teaspoon of cute baby Caydii
Sieve in a caring nannie
Pour in a loving me!

Fold together with kindness

Place in a nutty Auntie Claire (we call her Crunchy Nut)
Stir in a comedian Auntie Annie
Add a dollop of crazy Auntie Lol

Blend together with lots of hilarious jokes

A spoonful of smiley Carley
Sprinkle in mad Connor

Add a pinch of compassionate Uncle Jen

Mix it up to make it bonkers!

Broghan Griffin (9)
Manchester Hospital School, Manchester

Junkrat, Roadhog

Junkrat, junkrat,
Crazy, slender thief.
Whose cackle is contagious,
No one is his chief!

His eyes are orange lights.
Whizzing for any sign of gold
Approach him to find a face of fright!
Yet his bodyguard is more bold.

Roadhog, roadhog,
Balloon-like tattooed belly.
His deep voice grumbles,
But his leader talks all jelly.

Foggy eyes cover his gas mask,
With pointed shoulder guards as skyscrapers,
And a round ear-curling hook that echoes across the city.
Roaming like a zombie as if Frankenstein's his creator!

And with one less leg and an uncovered face,
Skilfully patrolling through the cities.
Planning all sorts of crazy schemes,
Even to steal the Queen's prized rubies!

Jude Anderton (8)
Manchester Hospital School, Manchester

Friendship

F irst pour a cup of kindness into a bowl,
R emember to put a teaspoon of joy into the bowl,
I f you get sad add a dollop of cheekiness,
E very blob of fun needs a sprinkle of patience,
N ow add a handful of craziness and a pinch of care,
S prinkle some delicious and delightful love into your mixture,
H eat a cupful of help,
I nside your mixture pour some hot and spicy adventure,
P lace a dollop of fun into your mixture.

Emmie Narayn-Nicholas (8)
Manchester Hospital School, Manchester

Enderman

E vil Enderman loves to kill
N ight-time is when Enderman comes out
D aytime is when Enderman hates
E vil Enderman is taller than a house
R aiding Enderman loves knocking houses
M ean Enderman loves invading other people's things
A s sneaky as a spider
N ever go out during night-time.

Saharah Nabi (11)
Manchester Hospital School, Manchester

Creepy As A Creeper

Green as a grumpy frog
Weird as an advert
Mischievous as a puppy
Annoying as school
Noisy like they're getting hurt
Attacks like a creeper
Sad like a dog.

Pippa Jane Tierney (7)
Manchester Hospital School, Manchester

Down I Go

Every day I'm digging deeper,
Deeper to the end of the world,
I will sleep in a hole to stay away from the snoopers,
Creepers that come out in a whole moon,
I will build in the morning,
Build a cosy house for night,
And like I said, sleep in a hole for night,
As morning follows through I start digging,
Oops I slip, guess that's the end of my world.

Amy Walling (10)
Maryport CE Junior School, Maryport

Halloween!

Halloween is near,
Witches, spiders, webs appear.
Ghosts and spooks walk in the night
Waiting to give us a terrible fright!
Children in their fancy dress,
Looking to find a bell to press,
Hoping to get sweets and treats,
Walking up and down the streets.
Trick or treat?

Yasmin Benson (10)
Maryport CE Junior School, Maryport

Creatures Of The Night!

Running for my life,
Shadows through the night,
Using my sword to strike,
The creatures of the night,
I got such a fright,
I just need the light,
To get them out of sight,
To have a happy life,
Goodbye my life has gone,
I've just been struck by one.

Heidi Martin (10)
Maryport CE Junior School, Maryport

Bonfire Night

Hats, scarves and gloves on tight,
The bonfire is now alight,
Colours of red and orange glow bright,
Warming up the night,
Joyous laughter fills the crowd,
The sky is filled with colour and sound.
With a bang, pop and whizz
Our hearts are all of a tizz.

Morgan Hazlewood (10)
Maryport CE Junior School, Maryport

Spooky, Scary Skeletons

Spooky, scary skeletons will give you a fright,
Spooky, scary skeletons will kill you at night,
Spooky, scary skeletons are breaking down your door
Spooky, scary skeletons just want to party more.
Spooky, scary skeletons are always eating rice,
Spooky, scary skeletons will give a nice slice.
Spooky, scary skeletons you find them in dungeons,
Spooky, scary skeletons will cut you like onions.
Spooky, scary skeletons need a sacrifice,
Spooky, scary skeletons will cook you up like rice.
Spooky, scary skeletons love to kill you,
Spooky, scary skeletons always stick together two by two.
Spooky, scary skeletons banging on the floor,
Spooky, scary skeletons love an apple core.
Spooky, scary skeletons love to make rafts,
But when they are tired they love a good nap.
Spooky, scary skeletons always fight in war,
Spooky, scary skeletons want to kill a boar.

Kianoosh Moshiri Zavieh (8)
Mesne Lea Primary School, Worsley

Creepers

Steve, Steve, beware, beware.
The creepers are lurking out there.
Mine outside you may,
Just make sure you don't become the creepers' prey.
The creepers are trying to find you,
Don't go to sleep, they could eat you.
Hide under the bed,
Just don't come out, if they find you then you'll be dead.
Go to the Nether you still won't be safe,
There lurk ghosts and zombie pigmen that want to turn you into steak.
Get out of there quick
Just be careful it could be a trick
Go upstairs you hear a buzzing noise. It's OK it's a bee
But there's something else and it's TNT.
Now you are dead
And I'm sure I told you to stay under the bed.

Joshua Anthony Clarke (9)
Mesne Lea Primary School, Worsley

Herobrine Discovered...

I stomped on the Wither and I ran through the End,
I killed the Ender Dragon with all my fellow friends.
I came across something great,
Which made me look directly straight.
I just saw Herobrine
Who's scarier than Frankenstein.
I might just see his face
But his house is a big disgrace.
I'm just using my electra to glide above the ground,
But the blood-curdling Herobrine is nowhere to be found.
There is my friend Alex glancing at a Vex,
I know that it could lead to a lot of scary deaths.
I kill Herobrine on his bed,
And now he's seriously dead.
I run back to my cave,
But you should know something,
There's someone lurking beneath the grave...

Jake Lewis (9)
Mesne Lea Primary School, Worsley

The Nether!

Nether, the wonderful world of wonders.
Nether, how could you resist the wonderful monsters and pigs?
Nether, a place where you can't see the sun,
Nether, a place where you can't tell day from night,
Nether, where zombie pigmen can fight!
Nether, what are the dangers?
Nether, the portal made of obsidian.
Nether, the portal made of flint and steel,
Nether, where lava's a familiar face!
Nether, a way to get a holiday!
Nether, glowstone lighting your way.

Millie Wright (9)
Mesne Lea Primary School, Worsley

Minecraft Life

I went through the portal,
What did I see?
An ugly Enderman looking at me.

I tried to break the hard bedrock,
But it turned out it was impossible to break.

I set TNT off,
With redstone torches and my traps.

Diamonds and sticks put it together,
It turned out as a diamond pick.

Beware when you are slaying slimes,
Mini slime will come in time,
Before night.

Joshua Thomas Whitehead (8)
Mesne Lea Primary School, Worsley

Untitled

Beware, beware, there's a creeper over there,
When you fight Slimes they get smaller and smaller until they die.
Mining for gold it's a lot of work,
I walk through a portal, what do I see?
A creepy-looking Enderman looking at me.
I run through the Wither to get to the end,
Finally my quest is complete.
So much to complete,
I found my darling diamonds
Zombies, the fighting fools get everywhere.

Sienna Parker (8)
Mesne Lea Primary School, Worsley

The Wonderful World Of Minecraft

I'm going to tell you a little melody,
But TNT is highly deadly,
It will be like a creeper,
Into the ground deeper and deeper!
Endermen are very scary,
When you're with them you feel very airy,
So walk away, just you try,
But never, never look them in the eye...
Building can be such a treat
But just then you must retreat,
Mobs spawn and start to stare,
Will you move, will you dare?

Chloe Walmsley-Taylor (8)
Mesne Lea Primary School, Worsley

Anything Minecraft

I walk through the portal, what do I see?
A black, ugly Enderman looking at me.

So I'm walking down the cave, I do no more,
Than use my pickaxe and mine some ore.

If you go to the Nether and get tickled by a feather,
It means a ghast has come to steal your leather.

The lava is really very hot,
If you don't dare to touch it, you're like a baby in a cot.

Daniel Redman (8)
Mesne Lea Primary School, Worsley

Crafting Rhymes

Beware when you are slaying slimes,
Skeletons are fighting fools,
Never go to the Nether,
When you get Ender pearls it is best to go to the end,
You can easily kill them with some tools,
Beware there are zombies everywhere,
Zombies, zombies, beware there are pros everywhere,
Digging for diamonds, have good luck, I will be waiting right above,
Traps, traps, try a tripwire instead of a trap.

Heidi Louise Whitehead (8)
Mesne Lea Primary School, Worsley

I Can Build Anything

If I wanted to build a mansion
Minecraft is the place.
If I wanted to build a football stadium,
Minecraft is the place.
If I wanted to build a swimming pool,
Minecraft is the place.
Minecraft is full of amazing materials,
Stained-glass windows like rainbows,
Concrete powder like white salt flour,
Terracotta is as orange as the sun.

Aiden Joshua Parker (8)
Mesne Lea Primary School, Worsley

Water And Diamonds

(A diamante poem)

Water
sparkling, refreshing,
cold, glazing, freezing,
flowing faster, diamonds, enchanted
crystal, shimmering, dazzling,
reflecting, eye-catching
expensive.

Radiyah Tanvir (9)
Mesne Lea Primary School, Worsley

Mining In The Dark

Mining in the dark,
Creepers make me... jump,
Wherever I go they follow me slowly.
Running through the dark,
Never even telling me,
Never being able to blow
My eyes turn to snow,
When they blow,
You may fall down,
Whenever they're chasing me.
Go near an ocelot,
Creepers hate ocelots
Run away!

Farrah Mawers (9)
Mesne Lea Primary School, Worsley

Ender Portal

Still bored,
Making the Ender portal
Hour, hour,
Gotta train to be a knight,
Finally done, let's go,
Slay the scaly-winged beast,
There it is, a golden apple,
Get TNT and blow him up.
Never ever go to the Nether with a wooden sword
Take a diamond sword,
It doesn't matter if you fall and fall.

Ted Crank (8)
Mesne Lea Primary School, Worsley

Weapons And Armour

W ater
E nderman
A xe
P ickaxe
O bsidian
N ever brick
S hovel

A pples
N ever
D iamond

A dventure map
R edstone
M ining
O ne
U pdates
R edstone torch.

Ellie Brooks (9)
Mesne Lea Primary School, Worsley

Nether Land

Still tired while I was building my house.
I found a portal and went in it
I found lots of cool things like:
Creatures, tools, lava, chests and death.
I had a nice time but I had to go home
I tried to find the portal but there was no portal
So I stayed with all of the monsters.

Maria Staniecka (8)
Mesne Lea Primary School, Worsley

TNT Time

Slaying slime
Crafting crafting tables
Training on trees
Mining in mines
Never ever go to the Nether without a steel sword!
Night night, time to fight
Get my diamond sword, time to fight Herobrine
TNT, time to have fun
Creepy creepers in the darkness.

Zane Samuel Taylor (8)
Mesne Lea Primary School, Worsley

Who Am I?

Who am I?
I have purple eyes
I am tall
I have a huge mouth
I have black skin
I'm an Enderman.

Who am I?
I have a giant frown
I can blow up
I am small and green
I have four legs and no arms
I'm a creeper.

Theo Kavanagh (9)
Mesne Lea Primary School, Worsley

The Creepy Creepers

We know he's around when the creepers attack
Around the creepers was a blown-up track.
I saw a sack lying on the ground
But when I did, I heard a loud sound.
But then I knew the creepers were around
But maybe it was cows, when I heard that sound.

Chase Oliver (8)
Mesne Lea Primary School, Worsley

Nature

When you plant scented thyme
Make sure the weather is kind.
Next when you're moving logs,
Don't step in bogs.
Then take a water melon break,
With your chocolate chip cookies that would be great.
With your obsidian
Make a great den.

Amelia Pimlott (8)
Mesne Lea Primary School, Worsley

Hot Fire And Shivering Ice

Hot fire, hot fire, burning loud in the night,
Scorching flames, flying into drains,
Shivering ice, shivering ice freezing fat mice,
Glittering icicles hanging from the lights,
Boiling fire, boiling fire, running through the wires.

Alexa Noon (8)
Mesne Lea Primary School, Worsley

The Everyday Life

A dventurer's map
N ether rack
I ce
M ooshroom
A dventures
L ava
S quirting squid.

Sophia Nation (9)
Mesne Lea Primary School, Worsley

The Dangers Of Life

P arrots
O celots
R abbits
T NT
A rctic
L ava
S pawn.

Charlie Michelle Steele (8)
Mesne Lea Primary School, Worsley

Crafting

I really need a hand getting some sand
Watch out from that creeper it's making me feel weaker
Yes, I got the gunpowder, I shouldn't have left my stuff out there
Where's my crafting table? Ugh! I left it where I'm not able
Any nearby forest, I hope, so I don't have to look upon it.
Now I'm mining a tree; oh, there goes a piggy,
Now I'm in a village, oh please be a spillage!
Ah, look a blacksmith, standing by a monolith!

Elsie Manning (8)
Our Lady Star Of The Sea RC Primary School, Whitby

The Spooky Adventure

M ining through deep, dark caves,
I n the spooky black night,
N ow discovering ores, shiny and bright,
E meralds found amongst the glistening treasure.
C olourful wood placed down on the floor
R andom pictures, random walls,
A mazing houses need a door,
F urniture, furniture, that's what we need now!
T o the market we go to have some fun, wow!

Sam Cochrane (9)
Our Lady Star Of The Sea RC Primary School, Whitby

In The Minecraft World

We can build a house of mud
Or of bricks and strips of wood.
We can get some cows and sheep,
To make a bed in which to sleep.

In Minecraft World skeletons roam
Where scary zombies have a home.
We try to catch a dragon so
Into the darkness we do go.

Gold and lapis we will plunder,
In the pit shaft we go under.
Armed with diamond shovels bright
The creepers have us within sight.

William James Chesworth (10)
St Oswald's Worleston CE Primary School, Worleston

The Minecraft Poem

M y user name is Awesome
I love Minecraft, I hope you know
N ever dislike Minecraft or punishment will happen
E verybody likes Minecraft
C rying never happens in Minecraft, hope you don't
R ather than making a house make a base underground
A little bit of TNT would make it better
F orever we love Minecraft
T ogether forever love Minecraft.

Annabelle Elizabeth Wilkinson (8)
St Oswald's Worleston CE Primary School, Worleston

Minecraft And Furnace

Mining diamonds
Igniting TNT
Morning mining
Fighting Endermen
Crafting diamond swords
Rapid Ender Dragon
A nice home to live in
Fighting Endermen
Wither.

Squid
Amazing, adventurous
Swims, fool, strong
Best character, mob, weird,
Limping, ugly, deadly
Very big
Zombie.

Edward Matthews (7)
The Berkeley Academy, Wistaston

Mine It, Craft It

M ining is building, enchanting and different
I n anger the bad guys are fighting the good
guys
N ight-blue sky when you fight the bad guys
E ating when the characters are hungry
C rafting, if you play the game you will craft it out
R aining, when you finish the cave it will rain
A xe to chop down trees, then they fall down
F east when it is dark
T umble down when you are dead.

Jack Want (8)
The Berkeley Academy, Wistaston

Blocks In Minecraft

M ine like mad with a pickaxe
I n your world you can build anything
N ew blocks always clay or iron
E ven anything you dream you can build
C raft everything including blocks of steel
R espawning is survival
A creature is the best
F all into lava and you're dead
T o fight the Ender Dragon you need diamonds and a sword.

Jackson Drury (7)
The Berkeley Academy, Wistaston

Minecraft

M ob is really fun in Minecraft
I ce-breaking Steve smashes ice
N ever killing Ender Dragon
E nder Dragon flew like the wind
C ows ran very fast across the green grass
R ed stone sparkled in the darkness
A weird black and white cow fell over
F un fighting the Ender Dragon
T wo villagers fighting.

Maximus George Bebbington (7)
The Berkeley Academy, Wistaston

Acrostic Doom

M ining diamonds in a cave
I n my head going to sleep
N ine diamonds in my inventory
E at cakes in your house
C rashing diamonds around
R eady to fight the Wither
A t my house eating enchanted golden apples
F ighting Herobrine with my diamond armour and sword
T he Wither shooting wither skulls.

Oliver Wood (7)
The Berkeley Academy, Wistaston

Minecraft Poem

M ine underground with a shiny pickaxe
I gloo as cold as the Arctic
N ight-time, mobs come out and hunt you
E asily
C raft a wooden pickaxe or a sword
R un away from the mean mobs
A ttacking mobs that will kill you
F lat Enderman is back and it is a master
T NT can blow up and crash your game.

Seb Hadzik (7)
The Berkeley Academy, Wistaston

Spider

S tring they can make for a trap
P opping up at night, make sure you keep them in sight
I s a spider a dangerous mob?
D eadly, creepy legs that's why you don't keep them as a pet
E ight eyes that are red, if they see you you'll be the prey
R oaming, hissing, hurting and that's why they're dangerous.

Matthew Orgill (8)
The Berkeley Academy, Wistaston

Alex And Skeleton

(A diamante poem)

Alex
creative, smart,
walking, skipping, jumping,
digging, character, dangerous mob,
breaking, attacking, slim build,
creepy, white,
skeleton.

Jacob Condrey (7)
The Berkeley Academy, Wistaston

A New Day In Minecraft

M ining, mining day and night,
I nventing crazy new things as the day progresses
N ew things to do every day
E xplosions destroying
C reepers creeping in the night
R ivers shining in the light
A lex exploring new places
F lames bright and burning
T omorrow is a new day.

Caleb Edwards (7)
The Berkeley Academy, Wistaston

Good Or Bad

(A diamante poem)

Notch
brave, powerful,
enchanting, fuming, hoping,
creative, eating, destroying,
attacking, controlling, writing,
evil, mean,
Herobrine.

Ralph Preston (8)
The Berkeley Academy, Wistaston

Zombie And Steve

M ining in the deep, dark woods
I n the mossy enormous caves
N ear a deep closed cave
E asily Steve wakes up
C rafting like Steve does
R ed houses people build
A fter you're asleep zombies might come in your house
F ighting zombies do
T NT is what people explode.

Ben Hall (7)
The Berkeley Academy, Wistaston

Sporty

(A diamante poem)

Squid
funny, smart
swimming, running, fighting
enchanting character, boss eating
swooping, attacking, flying
deadly, ugly
Ender dragon.

Max Cosby (7)
The Berkeley Academy, Wistaston

Survive Or Burn

(A diamante poem)

Lava
hot, bright
glimmering, building, spreading
killing, overflowing, exploding
affecting, breaking, harming
red, explosive
TNT.

Xander Drakeley (8)
The Berkeley Academy, Wistaston

Minecraft Is Scary

M ining in deep, dark caves
I n brown, dark woods
N ext door are neighbours
E nder Dragon that hurts you
C rafting the blocks to blow stuff up
R ed, fears of the Ender Dragon
A patch of burnt-down houses
F ighting the scary creepers
T ables with cake on.

Joshua Hassall (7)
The Berkeley Academy, Wistaston

Be Careful In Minecraft

(A diamante poem)

Steve
smart, adventurous,
spiders, sneaky, woods,
night, miner, careful man
digger, builder, day
dirty, ugly
zombies.

Blake Swift (8)
The Berkeley Academy, Wistaston

To Stay Alive

M ining shiny ores
I ce makes you go slow
N ight-time is when mobs come out
E ating makes your hunger go off
C rafting weapons and armour
R unning makes your hunger go down
A ttacking mobs
F inding diamonds
T rees can drop apples from branches.

Zachary Woodward Davies (7)
The Berkeley Academy, Wistaston

Never Or Die

Terrifying Ender Dragon attacked the army
Fire's flames as fast as the volcano's lava
Ice stops you as fast as a tornado
People shoot your buildings down like you have done
Something that you haven't done
You go to jail when you have stolen something
Diamonds shine as bright as the sun.

Liam James Austin (7)
The Berkeley Academy, Wistaston

Mine And Craft

M ine until you find diamonds
I gloos are fun to build
N ight is bad because the
E nder Dragon can kill you
C rafting is fun
R un after cows and sheep
A village is great you can trade
F ight dangerous mobs
T rade with villagers.

Jared Scott (7)
The Berkeley Academy, Wistaston

Minecraft Is Fun

M ining is fun
I gloo building is fun
N ever dig down
E ver
C rafting anything in Minecraft
R aiding in Minecraft
A pple picking is fun
F ighting is fun
T ree cutting is fun.

Jamie Steven Dove (7)
The Berkeley Academy, Wistaston

Superhero

M inecraft is amazing
I ncredible Minecraft
N o breaking homes
E nd of game
C reate things
R emake things
A mazing Minecraft
F antastic Minecraft
T ime to build.

Luca Walker (8)
The Berkeley Academy, Wistaston

Amazing

M inecraft
bu I lding
mor N ing hunting
min E diamonds
C rafting
R ed stone digging
A ll killing Endermen
F ighting Endermen
T alk to friends.

Dominic McKenzie Hassall (7)
The Berkeley Academy, Wistaston

Girls And Boys

(A diamante poem)

Girls
Beautiful, popular
Bouncing, posing, pouting
Bows, make-up, football, gangster
Smelly, scoring, winning
Offensive, mean
Boys.

Leah Clarke (9)
Yew Tree Community School, Chadderton

Girls And Boys

(A diamante poem)

Girls
Gorgeous, pretty
Loving, caring, flirting
Make-up, high heels, smelly, ugly
Football, active, dirty
Muddy, sweaty
Boys.

Leah Shannon Taylor (9)
Yew Tree Community School, Chadderton

Land And Sea

(A diamante poem)

Land
Dry, fresh
Amazing, breathing, tickling
Cool, nice, shiny, waves
Glittering, shining, shimmering
Wet, sparkly
Sea.

Tayyibah Ali (9)
Yew Tree Community School, Chadderton

Night And Day

(A diamante poem)

Night
Clear, calm
Relaxing, sparkling, lighting
Moon, star, bright, clear
Stunning, shining, changing
Warm, cold
Day.

Jessica Maddock (9)
Yew Tree Community School, Chadderton

Girls And Boys

(A diamante poem)

Girls
Hot, flirty
Make-up, phone, bed, PJs
Fighting, running, sleeping
Boasting, giddy
Boys.

Lilly May Heathcote (9)
Yew Tree Community School, Chadderton

YOUNG WRITERS INFORMATION

We hope you have enjoyed reading this book – and that you will continue to in the coming years.

If you're a young writer who enjoys reading and creative writing, or the parent of an enthusiastic poet or story writer, do visit our website **www.youngwriters.co.uk**. Here you will find free competitions, workshops and games, as well as recommended reads, a poetry glossary and our blog.

If you would like to order further copies of this book, or any of our other titles, then please give us a call or visit **www.youngwriters.co.uk**.

Young Writers
Remus House
Coltsfoot Drive
Peterborough
PE2 9BF
(01733) 890066
info@youngwriters.co.uk